Outside My Door

By Karla Nasser

Scott Foresman
is an imprint of

Glenview, Illinois • Boston, Massachusetts • Mesa, Arizona
Shoreview, Minnesota • Upper Saddle River, New Jersey

Photographs
Every effort has been made to secure permission and provide appropriate credit for photographic material. The publisher deeply regrets any omission and pledges to correct errors called to its attention in subsequent editions.

Unless otherwise acknowledged, all photographs are the property of Pearson Education, Inc.

Photo locators denoted as follows: Top (T), Center (C), Bottom (B), Left (L), Right (R), Background (Bkgd).

Cover: ©Greg Pease/Getty Images; **Title Page:** ©Lego/Getty Images; **3** Getty Images; **4** ©Dana Hoff/Beateworks/Corbis; **5** ©Thomas Barrat/Shutterstock; **6** Dario Lo Presti/ Fotolia; **7** ©Greg Pease/Getty Images; **8** ©Lego/Getty Images

ISBN 13: 978-0-328-39734-1
ISBN 10: 0-328-39734-2

Do you see the house?

Do you see the porch?

Do you see the yard?

Do you see the tree?

Do you see the fence?

Do you see the bike?